Soulful Liberation

By:

LaSheryl Davis

AARON PUBLISHING

This is a real story portraying the graphic details of pain and suffering experienced by domestic abuse victims. Mature reading audience suggested.

Printed in the United States of America

First Printing, July 2016

ISBN 978-0-692-75759-8

Aaron Publishing

PO Box 1144

Shelbyville, TN 37162

Dedication

To my Motivation, you have always been my reason to stand against the world that was pushing violently against me. We didn't have the beginning we would have wanted, the middle was filled with unwanted events as well. Nevertheless, I met a Savior that reconciled us back together. I carried you in my spirit before I even realized it. That was the one place no one could ever take you from, our secret place. When I didn't love myself enough to hang in there I always thought about you. Picturing your face was more than enough motivation to keep standing, to keep moving forward. My Motivation opened the door to my determination. I was determined that you wouldn't feel the affects of the pain I endured. I hope that now you see your past does not have to control or destroy your present and future. My Motivation, My Son, I have loved you from the moment I knew you were there. I'm honored to be your Mother.

Foreword

When I was asked to write the Foreword for this book, of course, I was honored, but honestly, I was extremely nervous as well. I've never done anything like this before and I didn't know if I could properly express how I feel about the book and the author, LaSheryl, who just happens to be my little sister. You see over the years I've had the privilege of doing life with Sheryl. I've seen her bad days as well as her good days. We've walked through situations of life and death together. I remember many nights praying and believing that one day she would find Truth. The Truth of who God is and who God created her to be. The Truth about who and what real Love is. The Truth about her value and worth. I knew that when she encountered this Truth that her life would change and she would never be the same and this is exactly what happened. As you read this book of her life's journey, I encourage you to think about your own life. Think about where you were, where you are now and where you want to be in the future. Although LaSheryl's past included emotional, mental and physical abuse, she didn't let it stop her. After making a life-saving decision to not die in the abuse, She began her new journey to Life. She took the time to learn the Truth about her identity and the One who created her. After surrendering her life to Jesus Christ, Sheryl realized that she was no longer a victim but a conqueror. She learned that the love of the Heavenly Father was everlasting and unconditional. Upon receiving her deliverance and freedom, she made a choice to share her story with others. No longer would her voice be silenced, she has something to say and this book is that voice. Her voice, her journey, her healing, her life. I'm so proud of the amazing woman of God that she has become. Her strength amazes me. It takes a strong person to openly share their healed scars but an even stronger person can identify the source of their wounds. I love you Sheryl and know that this book which was part of your liberation will empower others to pursue their own Soulful Liberation. I'm praying that God will heal and bless all that read it.

Love you to Life,

Patrice Tate

Exposing the darkness always releases The Light!!! That is exactly what LaSheryl has done in her first book. Soulful Liberation will cause you to look at the essence of freedom and bondage. I believe this book will become the workbook for women who are in abuse, have been abused and those who refuse to leave others in abuse. I have always known that God would take her misery and cause it to become her ministry. Soulful Liberation will indeed liberate your soul. I await the workbook and sequel.

Blessings Sweet Lady!!

Pastor Glenda Gleaves Sutton,

Senior Pastor of Family Affair Ministries

Fellowship, Nashville, TN

Table of Contents

Chapter 1

Liberty

Chapter 2

Pieces of Me

Chapter 3

Spirit Fuel

Chapter 1

Liberty

Shredded Memoirs

Writing was my way of escape. It was a way to release everything I was holding in. Though I struggled with where to put the correct punctuations, it didn't stop me. Reading short stories made me question if it's normal for mine to be my real day-to-day life, but that didn't stop me. Writing makes me free!

Even if I never share them with anyone, I'm still free. Notebook after notebook, I'm free. My everyday trials give me more to write about. The hitting, the kicking, and beatings didn't seem to stop me either. Writing makes me free! I'm trapped in hell, yet I'm free. I'm an adolescent punching bag, yet I'm free. I'm an everyday loser in a kickboxing match, yet I'm free.

I take beatings worse than meat being prepared for dinner, yet I'm free. Another beating, another story. Writing makes me free! It lets me escape the torture, the hell, I live in. I must hide my notebooks from the world. Though my world consists of only myself and one other person, my notebooks must stay hidden. Writing makes me free! Oh no! The dictator of my world, my protector, my lover, my abuser, found my notebook. He's putting a voice to my words, my inner thoughts, trapping my freedom. How? How did he get it? The hitting, the kicking, and the beatings he will give me now is nothing compared to the hitting, kicking, and beating I'm giving myself as I hear his voice release my words. My freedom is trapped. Writing was my way of escape. Now my short stories have become *"Shredded Memoirs"*........

Insight

I have a burning desire to write, but due to past experiences, I would always rip up my writings for my own safety. As a teen I was in a domestic violence relationship and my way of escape was writing. After one of those daily beatings, he went to sleep and I snuck in the bathroom to write and cry as always. Only this time I forgot to hide my notebook before I fell asleep. I woke up to him pushing and punching me in my arm saying, "What is this? Get your ass up! What is this?" With my eyes hardly open, I looked and saw my notebook. Every excuse I could think of began to flood my mind until the simple thought, "He is going to kill me flooded them all." In my pause, his anger grew worse. All I could say was, "I don't know—you tell me." He said, "It's your writing." As he began to read it out loud, I knew this was going to be bad.

What he was reading was me writing about a dream I had the night before. In the dream, he beat me, as he always did, but this time, it almost took my life. I expressed that I knew at some point I would be the one that would end up killing him. As much stuff as he did to other people, I knew I would be the one. It would be done with one of the many guns he had and I would wake up to them pointed in my face. As he finished reading the letter I tried to position myself in a way that I could jump up and run for cover. To my surprise, he didn't do anything. However, he made up a new rule; from now on I had to go to sleep either before him or with him, even if I wasn't sleepy. I tried to tell him it was a short story I made up, but he didn't believe me. He took my notebook (which crushed me) and told me to lay down. He said, "Go to sleep and don't get up until I get up." Of course, I said, "Okay." I laid there terrified, but more hurt that I wouldn't get my notebook back. He put his arm around me and I laid there looking at the ceiling.

The next morning when he told me to get up, I went to the bathroom thinking everything was okay. To my surprise, when I came out of the bathroom, he was sitting on the bed holding my notebook. I knew this was bad! He said, "So you're going to try and kill me?" I nervously reached to hug him and softly say, "No, it was a short story." He quickly jumped up yelling, screaming, and calling me all kinds of names. At this point, I'm holding my head down, twirling my fingers, mumbling what I assume are words. I tried to give myself a motivational speech as he began to circle around me, waving my notebook and yelling loudly. I'm telling myself, "Don't cry, you know it makes him angrier. Don't cry, only punks cry. Don't fall no matter how hard he hits or punches you. Don't fall! If you fall it will only make him angrier. Don't fall! The kicks hurt worse. Oh no! Sheryl, you're crying. Sheryl, hurry up and wipe your tears before he sees them or worse sees you move." Too late he saw both.

As he positions himself to punch me, he screams, "Bitch, what are you crying for?" That also gave him enough time to notice I wasn't in the proper position. The proper position was to stand straight up and put my hands behind my back. I instantly did it. When I took the first punch, I kept telling myself to survive. While my heart was breaking, even more, it whispered, "I'm only fourteen. Why me? Snap back, Sheryl, you can't survive being emotional." I took the first punch. The second punch rocked me, but I didn't fall. I guess that made him mad because the third punch knocked me backward off my feet. My body wanted to stay down, but my mind said, "Get up and survive!" I jumped up, stood straight up and put my hands behind my back again. The yelling and cussing continued along with the punches. At some point in the beating, I got confused. I learned no matter what, I was to stay in standing position, but he pulled me down to the floor by my hair. He kicked me over and over until his leg got tired. After all, that he told me to get up and get back in position. "Lord, when will this be over?" I wondered. No matter where he was at I had to keep facing him and obeying his orders. Then it happened; he had his back to me, turned around, and hit me so hard that I flipped over the bed. I laid there knowing this was how I was going to die. He pulled me up by my hair, still yelling, still screaming. I stood straight up with my hands behind my back as he mugged my face, pushing my head into the wall. He did that once and backed away. However, I stood there frozen. I was trying not to acknowledge all the pain I was in. He calmly said, "Go to the bathroom and clean yourself up." As I walked by him, sitting on the edge of the bed, he said, "You know I do this because I love you. If you kill me no one will love you." I said, "I know."

I went to the bathroom, cut the water on as loud as possible, and silently cried. He yelled, "Don't take too long." I mumbled lightly, "Okay," as I covered my mouth to stop the screams of my pain. I jumped, when he opened the door, in fear that he heard my crying. He said, "I was just checking to make sure the door wasn't locked and hurry up." I quickly came out behind him. He told me to get him something to drink and clean up the room so we could lie down. I did exactly what he said. He lies on his stomach, while I lie on my back looking at the ceiling. He put his arm across my chest so I couldn't get up. I don't know what hurt more, my body from all the hitting, punching, and kicking or my heart from having to lie there beside him. Either way, I was hurting. What does my future hold? Another guaranteed beating? Will I survive? Who knows? He went to sleep like everything was fine, while I stayed awake. When he woke up I acted like I had just woke up too.

I hated that room, but even more I hated the fact that everyone had to come through there to go to the bathroom. I knew they saw the holes in the wall. I also knew they knew those holes came from my body. How can people keep a secret that the walls are telling?

The Undelivered Letter

I'm sitting here watching the Tina Turner movie "What's Love Got To Do With It?" I'm wishing I used to get beat like her; at least she had a chance to run. Rooms are never big enough when you're running for your life. You start off running, knowing he is going to catch you, but a few minutes without the force of his fist hitting your body feels like a lifetime. I wonder what makes you hate a person so bad to beat them like that. What comes to mind is one of the four times he threw me across the room. Maybe that's why I'm afraid to fly. Though I never had physical bruises, my insides were bruised, beaten and battered. The one time my family called the police after a public beating, the police said they couldn't see any bruises or handprints. I remember every beating, like it just happened. As much as I try to bury them, they keep digging themselves up. I guess that's what happens when you try to bury stuff that is still alive; you think the dirt will suffocate it, but all it actually does is build up until it's rumbling out like a volcano. I can't bring myself to roll the stone. How can I forgive this man when I can't even face who I was then? I call myself "burying the horrible memories," but it wasn't the only thing that went in that grave.

My nickname was Fruity. Even though he didn't give me that name, he called me that for many years. Now many years down the road, I'm a mess trying to find myself. I didn't know who I was, I had no identity because he killed Fruity a long time ago. So who am I? For years I thought I was okay until I realized the memories never died and I needed Fruity to take her mess to the grave with her. So really, Fruity is not dead, because those memories are actually keeping her alive. I know if I get this stuff out and deal with it, then I can truly put it to rest. Then it will lose power.

How can I forgive him if I can't admit it happened?

So many things on the inside of me and people in my life saying I shouldn't be doing this, yet I know this has a greater purpose than I or anyone else will ever understand. When you're in the midst of tornadoes it's hard to pinpoint the starting point. I guess it would be easy to say, "the beginning," but who knows where that is? Some say there are always warning signs, but what happens when the warning comes with the action?

I knew all the stuff you were doing to other people, but it didn't bother me; especially when you were defending me from being sexually assaulted. To me, you were my own protector because he didn't bother me when you were around. Out of nowhere you just stopped coming around, leaving me in that nightmare all by myself. Hearing from you was bittersweet because you said you would be gone for awhile. I knew being left on my own was going to be horrible. When you came back around I was okay again because I had the dude I loved and he protected me. I remember how fast and crazy things started getting. All your run-ins with the dude on my behalf were fine with me. You just kept getting locked up and leaving me out here with no protection. Part of me felt like my plan backfired as if he was bothering me more to get back at you, while you weren't around. Either way, I had no one to run to, at least that's how I felt. The next time I saw you I had my son.

I remember all the times I would meet up with you at the fair. It would be fun for a minute until one of y'all would get into it with somebody and tell me to leave. I still remember all the times you would call or come by after the conflict and I sat there and listened no matter how bad it was, never once thinking you would be like that towards me. Honestly, I loved the gangsta in you. I remember when you called late one night saying you wanted to see me and talk and we stayed off of Harding Place. I got up and waited by the door to sneak outside to meet you. You looked nice with your brown two-toned sweater on. I sat and listened as you told me about your latest gun battle, raising your hand and showing me what had happened when the gun backfired on you. I got something to clean it up as we sat there a little longer. None of what you said bothered me at all. My mom only heard stories of you and didn't want you in her house. Summer days were hard sitting on that porch. She felt sorry for us one day and finally let us in the house. I remember your mom having to take me to see you at the justice center because I wasn't old enough to go on my own. Some stuff I saw you do, some stuff you told me about, but either way I turned a blind eye and deaf ear to it. The hardest thing for me was when that gangsta I loved turned on me. I'll never forget it, we were at your mom's house arguing, you pushed me down and began kicking me over and over. I laid there thinking, this is not supposed to be happening. I know the only reason you took me to the hospital was because you thought I was pregnant. That's the day I learned there were consequences for making you mad. When we found out I wasn't pregnant you were furious. I think at that point you either forgot or it just didn't matter that we loved each other. We argued and argued until you began screaming in my face. All I could think about was, he is supposed to love me, he isn't supposed to be acting like this towards me. The arguing went screaming and the screaming went to you slapping me. If stomping me wasn't bad enough, now you slapped me. While I was still full of courage and confidence I gathered my stuff to go. I was at the door, why did I let you stop me and listen to that apology? The decision I mad in that moment set the stage for what was ahead.

After that, it's hard to find a starting point because the beatings came more often, to the point they were a daily thing. Where do I start? Do I start at the time you kept punching me in the head because I was late picking you up for work when you were on work release? Do I start at the time you were beating me in the bathroom and knocked me down in the tub because your friend told you I was being smart with him? Do I start with the time you were hitting me so hard you knocked me over your mom's bed, landing between there and the wall (which seemed like the safest place at the time), then pulling me up by my hair? Do I start with the times you would put me out of the car late at night in the middle of the nowhere and leave me? Do I start with the time you beat me because I gave you the phone when a female called you? Do I start with the time you beat me because dinner wasn't ready? Do I start with the time you beat me, stomped me and threw me around the room when someone told you I was talking about your mom? Do I start with the time you kept hitting me in the head over at my cousin's house because I didn't want to go fix your plate of food, all the time fighting back tears acting like everything was okay? Do I start with the time you tried to run over me while I was carrying my cousin's baby? Do I start with the time you came by the house, threw a soda in my face, threw my boots at me, and tried to push me down the steps? Do I start with the times you would come to where I was and pull pistols on me and those I was with? Do I start with the time you saw me in the old projects and started hitting my head up against the bricks? Do I start with all the times you choked me and pulled my hair? Do I start with the time you shot my family? Do I start with the time you came to the house kicking doors and windows, yelling with two pistols in your hands? Do I start with the time we broke up and you saw me with someone else, beating me like your worst enemy? Do I start at the time you were shooting at me and your cousin told me I better get away from you before you kill me? Do I start with all the holes you put in your mom's walls with my body? Do I start with the child fighting and screaming to hold on to me because she knew you were about to beat me? Where do I start? How could I forget?

What better place to start than where you always did; with me standing up and putting my hands behind my back. Only this time I'm standing up to you, to tell you that I forgive you. For all that you've done to me, I forgive you. For every horrible, disre-spectful word you ever said to me, I forgive you. For every hit, push, slap, or kick, I forgive you. For every pistol you put in my face and every bullet you shot at me, I forgive you. For marrying you for the wrong reasons, I forgive myself. It turns out, I did know where to start, at forgiveness! I thought you took or beat all that I had out of me, but I was wrong—you were wrong. You never have to admit it because this is me forgiving you. May the Grace of God be with you!

Insight

The *"Undelivered Letter"* was one of the hardest letters I have ever written. No, it never made it to the person it was created for, but at least I got it out. I had the desire to write, but actually doing it came with too much baggage. At the time it was baggage I wasn't ready to deal with. I eventually found myself at a local church, which later became my church home. After being there a short time it seemed like my past caught up with me. Our Pastor always talked to us about journaling, but I was offended every time she said it. I took it personal as if she was talking only to me. I wondered how she knew; and if she knew, why would she have me journal. It took more time reading the Bible, listening to praise, worshiping, and spending time with God before I actually started journaling. In doing so I realized she was only trying to help us release what we weren't created to carry. When I did begin to write again, I think I shocked myself for awhile, but my next step was all too familiar. I was still ripping my writings up upon completion. I still celebrated myself for at least getting the words on paper. A few more years went by before I was able to start saving them. Once day I noticed how far back my journals were hidden in my closet. Although I lived by myself, I was still afraid of someone finding them. I was still not ready to deal with the fear, the hurt, and the pain of it all, so I kept them hidden. Even more years passed before I realized my writings had blessed the walls of my closet, encouraged my clothes, motivated my shoes, but did nothing for others. Now I'm setting them free so that I can truly be free.

Domestic violence is so much more than physical hitting. It's the emotional abuse that lasts long past the soreness of your body. It puts you in a place of disbelieving, confusion, and just a feeling of being lost. Day after day, beating after beating, you find yourself trying to figure out how it got to this point. How did it start? It was a constant battle because when he told me he beat me because he loved me, but I knew that couldn't be true. The only problem was now he had me believing no one else would love me. I even asked myself who would really love me knowing all I am was a human punching bag. Who would love me enough to keep me safe? Who could handle loving me without touching me because my body was so fragile from the beatings?

It's the verbal abuse that has you jumping every time a man raises his voice. Years down the road, many miles of distance between us; yet the side effects of him never left. This made it very difficult for me. For a long time when I would have a simple disagreement with a man and he raised his voice, I would shut down. It was like a warning that preceded a punch. I don't know what was worse the yelling or being called bitch and hoe all the time. It had to be the yelling;, simply because anger, hate, and evil accompanied it. It's the mental abuse which had you ready to die as a solution to all the pain. The mental abuse had me thinking this was my life until he decided to kill me.

I'm an adult still dealing with the effects of this teenage relationship. This is not normal or okay to be treated like this nor is it okay to treat someone else like that. If you are a loved one of someone going through it, please know your approach is very important. Don't assume the victim is staying because they are stupid or for some other reason; it may be because he threatened their loved ones if they leave. Tell her the opposite of what he is telling her. Reassure her she is valuable, that people love her unconditionally, and that it's not her fault. Let her know she has a safe place to come to. I guarantee he is telling her no one will help her, be there for her or love her like him. Help her rebuild everything he beat down. If you are the abuser, please don't let pride or shame stop you from seeking help to stop this destructive behavior.

My Friend

The pen is my friend. The paper is my best friend. I want to be married, but first, I have to end the affair with low self-esteem and divorce pain. I've been told, "It is okay to cry; it cleanses your soul." Yet I've been beaten not to cry. Along with those beatings came an aggressive lecture telling me that crying is for punks and shows weakness.

I want to write about happy things, but for every good moment, there are two bad ones to crush it. Maybe he was right when he said, "If leaving me will make you happy, then bitch you will never be happy." It's a hell of a thing to leave him and still be stuck with him. I want to cry, but a strength of fear won't let me. What does strength of fear mean you ask? "It's the strong fear of him finding out," I cried. Strong fear of being punched in the face for every tear that comes out. I thought only God is supposed to know how many tears you drop. When the next tear that falls will get you hit, you start keeping track of how many you can take.

While writing this time, what comes to mind is memorials. To me they can be both bad and good, depending on the memory. One of mine just happened to be a public display. Imagine how it must feel constantly riding by the place where you knew your life was about to end. Well, I do on a regular basis. Sometimes I force myself to look at it and other times I get mad because I feel like it should have been fixed or replaced by now. I wonder, "Do people know what happened to damage the property in that space?"

I was no longer in a relationship with him, but he refused to leave me alone. I couldn't understand why he was doing this to me? All I ever tried to do was love him. In return, I got back hate and violence. I can tell you, that night the unwanted memorial was created, I was ready for him to just kill me. He was stalking me, unbeknownst to me, and did not like what he saw. In the attempt to flee him and get to safety, he was chasing the car I was in. We were going down side streets, the main street, and even the interstate at a high rate of speed. The car I was in was being shot at with a 12 gauge shotgun, which was an indication I was probably going to die. His actions that night did not just affect me, but because I was a common denominator I felt responsible to a certain extent. I was tired of running! I couldn't run anymore! Just like another time he did the total opposite of what I expected of him. If all you do is conflict pain on me to hurt me, then why not finish it? I made it through that night, but it had horrible consequences. If it wasn't bad enough, I was blamed for it all. I was so scared, tired, and ready to give up, but somehow I didn't. I couldn't figure out who was tricking me, him or God?

While trying to exit the interstate the car I was in lost control and wrecked. Being that I was in the floorboard of the front passenger side, I didn't know what happened. I didn't know if he was still around or not. Then I heard him yelling, cussing, and sounding full of anger. I got out of the car and just ran. I didn't know where I was at or where I was running to. I felt like I was in a death scene of a horror movie. Just like in the movies trying to get away, I fell. I quickly jumped back up because I could tell that I hadn't made it far enough. I'm up running through the trees, trying to avoid being hit in the face by branches and it happened again. I fell, my legs were tired. I was hoping I had some good distance from him. I was wrong because I could hear his voice clearly. I got back up and started running again. I'm crying, screaming, "Somebody, please help me!" I hear him screaming, "Fruity, stop running, stop running." I cried out, "No, you're going to kill me." Then it happened a third time, I fell again. This time, I just stayed on the ground. I could tell by the sound of his voice, he was too close to get away. Once he approached me he said, "Come on before the police come. I said, "No! What did you do?" He just kept saying get up and come on before the police come. I said, "No! If you're going to kill me then you will have to do it right here." He said, "I'm not going to do anything to you." He grabbed my arm to pull me up. He said, "Let's go because if the police come I am going to kill you." As I see the car I was riding in, I looked inside and began yelling at him asking him, "What did you do?" Of course, he kept saying, "Nothing!"

He kept yelling at me to get in the car, but I said, "No!" He grabbed my arm with one hand and was still holding the shotgun in the other hand. Once he was heading to the driver side, I started walking backward away from the car. He immediately jumped back out and started coming towards me. He pointed the shotgun at me and said, "Get in the car." I jumped in the back seat while he was walking towards the driver side. I kept screaming, "I can't feel my legs; you shot me." He's yelling, "No, I didn't that's all that falling you were doing trying to run away from me." He was driving fast, crazy, yelling at me, and trying to reach for me in the back seat. Oh my goodness! He slammed on the brakes and put the car in park. I saw him reach to open his door so I jumped out on the opposite side. He was chasing me around the car saying, "Bitch, I'm going to kill you." I'm crying, asking, "Why? Why don't you just leave me alone? What did I ever do to you?" In the midst of my tears, I notice we are in front of one of my family members house. I began screaming at the top of my lungs. I was so angry thinking people are normally out all the time, so where are they now? He said, "If you keep screaming for them and they come out, I'm going to kill everybody in the house." I stopped screaming and asked him, "What do you want me to do so you won't hurt my family?" He said, "Get in the car." I got back in the backseat. He took us to hide the gun and bragged about what he had done. His cousin came to the car to check on me. He said, "If you don't get away from him, he's going to kill you." I looked at him with tears in my eyes and said, "I keep trying to, but he won't leave me alone. We are broke up now, but he acts like we are still together, plus he said he would kill my family."

When we go to his safe place I knew I had more to come. We were met at the door with screams and questions. "What happened? Tell me what happened," she said. He calmly looked at me and said, "Ask Fruity." I stood there frozen, knowing if I opened my mouth, to tell the truth he would probably beat me to death. The screaming and questions kept coming. He kept giving the same response, "Ask Fruity because it's her fault." She yelled at him, "Stop lying! I know you have done something." She said, "Fruity, sit down and tell me what happened." He said, "Fruity, stand up and don't say anything." This went on for what seemed like forever. Finally, she stood in front of him and said, "Fruity, tell me now what happened." He looked over her to look me in my eyes. I said, "It was my fault." He said, "Now get up and get in the room." She said, "You don't have to go in there," but I knew I did. My heart dropped as I made the turn to go in the room. I knew I could have possibly been taking my last steps.

He shut the door behind us once we got in the room. I stood there frozen, fumbling with my fingers. I held my head down trying to hide the fact I had been crying. He said, "You see what you made me do?" He lies down in bed like it was a regular night. I said, "You're right, it's my fault." I stood there as I always did, standing straight up with my hands behind my back. I didn't move until he told me to come and sit by him on the bed. I knew the punches were going to hurt sitting that close. He said, "You know I love you and if you wouldn't have made me do this, then none of this would have happened." I didn't respond until I was told to. Even then I agreed to whatever he said and took blame for whatever he told me.

At the beginning of this nightmare I had left a detailed note to inform my family of names, phone numbers, and who could show them directions. When I heard them at the front door I was screaming on the inside, "Please save me." I was so nervous because I didn't know how he would react to my family being there. He looked at me and said, "Don't leave me." I said, "I have to go." He grabbed my arm. I jumped, of course, trying to act like everything was okay. His family member is screaming, "Fruity, let's go! Your family is here." Oh my goodness, he said, "Don't move." I stayed still thinking it would protect family members standing at the door. He kept saying, "Don't leave me, don't leave me." I said, "Ok, I won't leave you, but I have to go with them tonight." He said, "Okay, but if you don't call or come back I'm going to kill your family." I said, "Okay."

I went to the police station to fill out the paperwork. I told them everything , but I wasn't totally confident that it would stop him. I just wanted to die or at least hide. I felt horrible, ashamed, and responsible for being the common denominator. How could I have brought this terrible problem in multiple people's lives? I didn't know what was worse, people blaming me or me blaming myself. I wanted to tell everyone who would listen that it really wasn't my fault. I wasn't even having contact with him. I don't know how or when he started following me to the different places I went. Either way, to me, no one wanted to hear what I had to say anyway. For a little while after this, I actually felt like I could breathe like I could finally relax. But, truthfully I knew it was only temporary. I knew if I didn't call him or go back to him that he would keep his word and kill my family. The only solution I had was to give him what he wanted, which was me. I was a teenager trying to figure out how to protect my family and keep myself alive. In my mind, it was better for me to keep taking the beatings instead of destroying the family.

I knew my body would eventually heal or he would finally

kill me. Either one of those was still better than the thought of my family hating me. I believed every threat he said because even if he didn't fulfill his threats he came very close to it. I went back knowing that more beatings were sure to come. I handled things the best way a teenager could or so I thought.

Memory Lane

<u>Memory 1-</u>

I remember when I got a job at the hotel and a male employee called me a bitch. I argue with the guy trying to make him apologize, but the situation got out of hand, so I decided to leave early. I called my boyfriend to tell him I was getting off early and why. He said, "Why did you let the guy call you a bitch?" I told him I was arguing back with the guy, but it wasn't good enough for him. He came up there, sat in the car with two lemon squeeze 9mm's in his hands waiting for the male employee to come outside. However, the manager hid the male employee in a safe place. When I told him they hid the guy he said, "You know because you let him call you a bitch and I had to come up here early, I'm getting you when we get home." I tried to explain how I tried to straighten the guy out, but he was still angry. When we made it home he stayed true to his word. Back into position I went. Standing straight up with my hands behind my back, taking punches to my body and face. I was begging myself not to let a tear drop or fall from one of the blows. Doing those two things only made things worse. No matter how strong I tried to stand, the blows were just too hard. I fell. He was kicking me like I was dirt (the kind of kicks when you lean back and come forward.) I just knew I had to get up because at least the punches didn't hurt as bad as the kicks. Plus, I would rather stand up on my own than being pulled up by my hair. This man beat me until he got tired, not just this time, but every time.

<u>Memory 2-</u>

I was working at a local fast food restaurant and I really enjoyed being there. Working gave me a break away from him. Not to mention when I got paid, I would give him money to get high. I know it sounds crazy, but while he was out getting high, I didn't have to worry about him bothering me. He took me to work one day, but the manager was right there when I got out of the car and said I couldn't work without my hat. I turned back to look and see if the windows were down on the car. Of course, they were and he heard my manager. I walked into the building with the manager to try and sneak around my boyfriend and ask him if I could please work. I told the manager I couldn't tell him to take me home to get my hat and bring me back. A female employee asked me, "Why can't you ask him? Is he hitting you?" I turned around to make sure he wasn't right there but noticed he was getting out of the car. I told her to please be quiet and not to say anything. He came in the restaurant and said, "Let's go! I heard what your manager said." I looked at my manager and began to walk out the door. Then manager and female employee heard him start yelling at me as he walked out the door in front of me. The manager said, "Tell him you can work without the hat," but I knew it was too late. I told the manager, "Never mind, it's too late." The manager asked me if he was hitting me? I then saw him coming back in, so I told the manager, "If he comes back in here, it's not going to be good." I tried to stop him at the door, but he pushed past me telling the manager it would be my last day. I was so hurt he had taken some-thing else from me. When we got in the car, he kept telling me to take off the shirt and give it back to them. I kept trying to explain that I didn't have a shirt on under it. He said, "Well, give me your nametag." He took it back in, said something, came back out and we left. The next time I went back there was because he needed to get high and wanted to know about my last check. I called to make sure my check was there. Once they confirmed it, we went straight there to get it. As I handed them the shirt and hat, the manager kept saying, "You don't have to go with him. We can get you some help." I said, "I can't do this. If I stay in here too long he will shoot everyone in here." When I got in the car he said, "What did the manager say?" I lied and said, "Oh, he asked me to come back to work, but I told him no."

Memory 3-

In the Undelivered Letter, I mention an incident about being beaten because he thought I talked about his mom. I remember walking into the house one day and I could tell something was wrong. The three people who were in the room were barely looking or speaking to me. They kept looking at each other, making faces while I was trying to be overly friendly. The first person walked out the door, but not before she made a smart remark. It didn't affect me because I didn't even know what was going on. It must have struck a nerve with him because he jumped up and said let's go in the room. The second person laughed as if something was funny. He laid in the bed as I sat by him casually talking. Out of nowhere the tone of the conversation changed. He said, "I know what you've done." With my puzzled face, I asked, "What did I do that you know about?" He aggressively kept repeating it, but I had no clue what he was talking about. I knew where this would end up, but I didn't even know why. The second person in the other room heard him yelling at me and she came in and told us she was leaving with a smile on her face. He said, "Okay." I sat there confused and speechless. When he heard the front door shut, he jumped up knocking me off the bed. I tried to get up, but he pushed me back down. I kept trying to ask him what was wrong, what he thought I had done. He wasn't listening to me. He kept yelling in my face, "Bitch, stop lying! I know what you have done and since you don't want to tell me, we will do this until you do." He kicked me in the chest and I went backward a little bit grabbing the bed for balance. Whatever it was he thought I did have him really mad and I couldn't calm him down because I didn't even know what it was. He just kept kicking me, calling me all kinds of bitches, telling me I was going to pay for what I had done and that I better hope he didn't kill me. I was trying to protect my face, but he moved my hands and started smacking my face. I think he must have got tired of bending down because he said, "Bitch, stand up!" I stood up for him only to have him kick me into the wall. As I fell to the floor I prayed the glass from the window didn't fall on my face. I wasn't worried about my face, just didn't want people to know how it broke. To my relief, it did not break. I got back up as if nothing happened. I stood there in pain clueless. I was taking punch after punch wondering when my body was going to give up. He noticed my hands were not behind my back and started twisting my arms yelling, "Bitch, I will break your arms! You know the position." I messed up and let a tear drop. He choked me up against the wall saying, "You want something to cry about?" I tried to shake my head no, but thought it might be better to let him choke me. He slung me to the middle of the floor. As I was being kicked to the other wall he said, "Bitch, you think you can talk about my mama and I won't do anything about it. Hoe, I will kill you!" He pulled me up by my shirt and had me standing against the door. I said, "I never said anything about your mom, I don't know what you're talking about." He punched me in the mouth and kept yelling, "You better tell me something." Every time I tried to open my mouth he hit me in it. The more I told him I didn't know what he was talking about, the more he pushed my head against the door. He slung me against the third wall in the room, repeating the same things he was doing on the previous wall. Then it happened! He slung me over the bed and my body hit the wall so hard. I thought, "I'm not going to survive; I know I'm not." As I laid there, he stood over me stomping on me as hard as he could. He pulled me up and slung me against the fourth wall. My body literally hit every wall in the room, yet somehow I was still standing. By this time, he was getting tired because he was yelling more than hitting. He finally told me what I had supposedly done. None of which was true. I begged him to give me time to prove it. He said, "Okay, but if it turns out you said it, next time I will kill you." He walked off leaving me standing there for thirty minutes; as if I was a child in time out. As always he told me to clean myself and the room up. Now it was time for me to clean up the mess he made while beating me. Pain and all, I cleaned the room like nothing ever happened.

The next morning when he let me get up, I started calling around to get things settled. By the time I got to the person who could clear everything up, she had an attitude. I tried, nicely, to tell her what was going on and she very smartly replied, "I don't care about your boyfriend or his people. I've got better things to do." I told her I understood, but it was causing serious problems. She finally said what was needed to clear my name. He was sitting right there listening to it all and I told her thank you and hung up the phone. When everyone came back to the house he told them what really happened. They laughed and said, "I knew Fruity wouldn't do anything lie that." I couldn't figure out what was so funny. "What exactly were they smiling about?" I wondered because the beating was not funny. There was no apology that could be given to erase what he did to me. It didn't matter, though, he never planned on giving me an apology.

To make things even crazier I never saw the person who started all of this trouble again until years later. I must admit I was shocked when I saw her, but not excited. I was polite but irritated she wanted to talk as if everything was lovely between us. On the inside I was praying, "Holy Spirit, bring back to me the remembrance of Your Word! Remind me of Your Love, Grace, Mercy and mostly Forgiveness!" I thought maybe it showed on my face, but I know God is an on-time God and He knows when it's time to release and heal. She said, "I'm sorry. I knew what was going on; we all knew what he was doing to you, but we never stopped it." I asked her, "What are you apologizing for when his the one who did it?" I was waiting for her to apologize for that one particular incident she had caused, but it never came out. As she stared at me blankly, I first repented in my spirit of unforgiveness and then peacefully told her she didn't have to keep apologizing. She said, "I feel so sorry for you." I joyfully replied, "You don't have to feel sorry for me. He is the one who was and is full of anger. Yes, all that stuff and more happened to me, but by the Grace of God I made it out. I didn't know it then, but for God to bring me through that situation it had to be for a Greater Purpose! I'm blessed beyond measure and if God did if for me then, I know He can and will do it for you. Needless to say, she was now the shocked one. I walked away proud that I heard the voice of the Lord and was obedient. I had faced a part of my past which had haunted me for years. This may seem small to some, but it was a Victory for me; plus I did it humbly and gracefully. I know everything has levels to it, but this one has been conquered. Now it's on to the next one. It may not happen in the timing you want it to, but it will happen in the timing of the One who created time. Make sure you're in the place to hear Him and obey what He says. This is accomplished by allowing Jesus Christ into your heart and life as your Lord and Savior. No, this doesn't mean everything will be peaches and cream, but it will be done in peace, love, grace and so much more as long as you stay in Him, His Word, and His Presence.

After my ex was no longer around, I tried everything to deal with the hurt he and other things had caused. I tried drinking the pain away, sexing the pain away, and I even tried suicide. None of these things worked. I thought on top of all the things that had happened to me as a child and teen, I couldn't even control the pain away. Everything I tried only made me feel worse; until I encountered Jesus.

Memory 4-

I think about the time he was on work release and I was late picking him up. I had the car and some free time away from him, so I decided to go see my cousin. I hung out with her for awhile. We drove to my mom's house and while I was there he paged me to tell me they were letting him off early. I said, "Okay," and told my cousin to come on so I could drop her off. I knew it would take me almost an hour before I could pick him up. When I made it to him, I saw him sitting in the dining room. He got in the car without saying a word. I kept asking him where we were going, but he wouldn't reply. I just drove to his normal hangout spot. While in route there, we were approaching a stop sign and he began to yell at me, asking where I had been. I kept trying to remind him about having to go to my mom's house. He replied, "That shouldn't have taken so long." I couldn't tell him about being with my cousin. I hadn't asked him if I could go over to her house and have her ride with me. He was so angry with me by the time I stopped at the stop sign, he punched me in the head. I released a slight scream while trying to fight back the tears. I asked, "Why did you hit me while I'm driving?" His only response was, "Because you were late, they were letting me off work and I would have had more time before I went back." He punched me again. I responded, "If you keep hitting me I won't be able to drive." I noticed a man standing on the sidewalk looking in the car. The man leaned down and said, "Don't hit that girl again." With my eyes full of tears, I told the man, "No, please don't try to help me." The man kept saying, "Don't hit that girl again." He looked at the man and asked, "Nigga, what did you say?" I kept telling the man, "Please, walk away." I grabbed my boyfriend's arm trying to stop him from grabbing his gun. Of course, that made things worse. The consequence for this was being punched three times, back to back. Once my head steadied out I quickly drove off. I didn't want him to hurt that man who was simply trying to help.

It is sad to say I have many more memories similar to these. Part of the deception domestic violence holds is that it never starts off like this. Looking back on things I definitely know mental abuse led to emotional abuse, which led to verbal abuse then to the part everyone sees from those three levels, physical abuse. My mind could not figure out how the man who protected me turned into my abuser. How was his love for me the reason he beat me? I was asked by one of his family members, "Do you still love him?" I said, "No; he beat the love out of me." Every attempt to leave was a failure with painful consequences. I learned how to survive. I gave him what he wanted when he wanted it. I was totally programmed. He controlled my mind. Do you know how twisted your mind is when someone you love beats you and says they did it because they love you, while telling you no one will love you like them? To this day, I can't unweave the web of it all, but especially the mental abuse. If someone can get your mind, they have you.

<u>Memory 5-</u>

My day was going surprisingly good while out shopping with his mom. She bought me an outfit, but I knew I would probably never get to wear it. He picked out my clothes and told me what to put on every day. I showed him the outfit and he liked it. He said he was going to the store and he would bring me something back. Hours went by without a phone call or snack of any kind. Some of my cousins popped up asking me to go out with them. I kept saying no because he wasn't there for me to ask him. His mom said, "Girl, get out of the house and as a matter of fact, wear the outfit I just bought you." I was excited, got dressed and we left. We made it to the club we were going to. After a while of being there, one of my cousin's male friends said, "Let's go to the store." When we got back to the club we decided to sit in the car and talk. My cousin, sitting up front, said, "Sheryl, get down! I think I saw your boyfriend drive by." I immediately slid down in the seat, but still tried to look out the window. We saw headlights approaching us, so we all slid down even more. My cousin's male friend kept saying, "I'm not getting down, I'm not scared of him." I replied, "Please, get down." We were all quiet as he drove by us. Once he turned the corner, we snuck back to our car, so they could take me home before he got there. We pulled up to the house, I jumped out of the car and ran in the house. His mom said, "Did he catch you?" I said, "No, but almost." I kept looking outside to make sure my cousins pulled off quickly, but they were still sitting there. I heard voices and footsteps coming closer to the door. He walked in and said, "Here is your snack and look who's here." I acted surprised to see my cousin standing there. He said, "They were pulling up the same time as me and want to know if you can go out with them?" He said, "Go get dressed, you can go." I ran into the other room and slipped off the gown I had on to cover my clothes. When I got back in the car with my cousins, we all busted out laughing. The next morning was confusing as ever. When I got up he kept asking me what I did at the club. I replied, "Just listened to music." He asked, "Did you drink?" My pause was all the answer he needed. He gave me a back-handed slap and said, "Don't ever drink again. I told you that you could go out, but I didn't say you could drink." I said, "Okay," and sat there until he told me to get up and cook lunch.

I would like to be able to say all of this chaos stopped on this particular date, but it wouldn't be true. The effects of the abuse stayed with me for years and affected my life on a daily basis. Any relationship I attempted to get into or had suffered from abuse it knew nothing about. In some way, this man always found out where I worked, my phone number and my address. Because of that, I moved every year, changed my number every six months (more if needed), and took security measures at work. I remember one time he called me unexpectedly. As soon as I heard him say, "Fruity..," I sadly asked, "Why won't you leave me alone?" His constant threat of killing me and thought of him going to the penitentiary for trying pops in my mind from time to time wondering what would happen when he gets out. It's this torture I longed to be free from. I'm glad to say throughout the years I have stopped moving, changing my phone number and stopped setting up security measures at work. I grew tired of living in that fear. I was ready to laugh and live my life in freedom. I learned that it was so much easier said than done. I made mistakes, but I also learned a lot and accomplished personal goals. Most of all I allowed the Lord to minister to me; restore within me what the devil thought he took, and rebuild what was broken down teaching me "Who and What" Love really was. It's an every day, every hour, every minute, every second battle to choose to walk in the Truth of Christ concerning life. Some areas have become easier, but other areas have levels to them. Two of the scriptures I use to fight this battle are 1 John 4:8-19 and Galatians 5:1. I believe there is no such thing as a small or big victory; victory is victory, either way. I purposely celebrate each level I accomplish and issue I overcome. I no longer deal with these memories from a place of fear and bondage, but a place of strength and freedom.

Memory 6-

It was a summer night and I had decided to switch cars with someone. Unbeknownst to me, the person I switched cars with switched my car again with a third person. I went to clubs as we always had. I really enjoyed myself too. When I woke up later by panicking people I was very confused. They were pushing me saying, "Get up! You have to go! He's looking for you." I kept saying, "What? Who?" They said my ex had shot my family member and was looking for me. I was so very hurt. Apparently while I was at the club, my ex was riding around looking for me. When he located my car, he knocked on the door assuming I was in there. From what I was told, when they asked him his name he gave them a fake one. My family member recognized his voice but didn't open the door. The gun could be heard being cocked through the door.

My ex shot through the door hitting my family member in the back. All praises to God they survived. I didn't get a chance to tell them I was sorry, that I wished it had happened to me. My family made a plan to relocate me to another city. Since I had to leave immediately and I wasn't allowed at the hospital, I wrote my family member a letter. I worried about whether or not they got the letter. I began receiving threatening messages from other family members. However, it was an ass whooping I was willing to take. I felt like it was all my fault. I just wished it was me instead of an innocent person. I thought maybe I shouldn't let them hide me, but rather turn myself over to him; letting him finish killing my body since my insides felt already dead. While I was in the new location word was given to me to call him. I was hesitant at first until I was told it involved two other family members. When I called him, the first thing he said was, "If I wanted to get to you, I could because I know where you're at." I didn't believe him until he told me where I was and who told him. I was shocked again. I asked him why he did what he did. He just kept saying, "Bitch, I was trying to kill you." He had no remorse at all. I replied, "What was so important that I needed to call you?" He began to tell me how he had been seeing two of my family members riding in his hangout spots, but how they had not seen him. He wanted me to tell them to stop before he killed them. I begged him not to. I hung up trying to figure out how to escape this nightmare. I called one of my family members to tell them what he said. I begged this person to stop. I couldn't handle any more guilt and shame. They agreed to stop.

Memory7-

I asked him if I could go to my mom's house to visit and babysit my nephew. He said, "Yes." The next morning he called to see what I was doing. I told him I was feeding the baby and watching TV. He heard my mom talking in the background, so he told me to come back over there and let my mom watch the baby. I said

I wanted to spend some time with him, but I didn't have a ride. I heard his niece and nephew in the background and asked what they were doing. He said, "Nothing, I'm babysitting them." I said, "Well we both are babysitting so you will have to see me later." His tone changed and started getting angry. He kept saying, "Stop playing and come over here." I just hung up. I figured by now he knew where my mom had moved to, but he didn't have a car. My mom asked me who kept calling? I told her not to worry about it, I'd handle it. I cut the ringer off, then maybe thirty minutes later I heard my mom scream, "Who is this?" I jumped out of bed, ran into the living room and saw a car parked between the grass and the driveway, angled toward the house. I didn't recognize the car so I replied, "I don't know." We didn't see anyone get out of the car so my mom started walking around the house looking out the windows. We heard banging on the back bedroom window. We ran back there because that was where my nephew was sleeping. My mom said stay back here on the floor so he can't see you. I picked up my nephew, who was only a few months old, and sat on the floor beside the bed. I could hear my mom yelling, "What do you want?" He kept saying, "Tell Fruity to come outside." My mom argued with him, but I knew this was a dangerous thing to do. I laid my nephew on the floor so I could crawl to the phone. My mom told me to take the baby in the bathroom away from the windows. I told her to come in there with us, but she said, "No." She said she was going to distract him away from us while I called the police. I called the police and told them what was going on. The operator asked all the normal questions and I gave all the normal answers. She asked if he was known to carry any weapons. I said, "Yes, two lemon squeeze 9mms." She said, "What does that mean?" I replied, "Well, he says all he has to do is squeeze the trigger one time and it will keep going." She responded, "I'm letting the officers know all of this." She asked what kind of car he had. I replied that I didn't know who's car was there because he didn't have a car. I felt like someone would definitely be hurt before the police made it there. I told the operator I was going to give my mom the baby and go outside so he would leave. The operator insisted I didn't and told me the police would be there shortly. I could still hear my mom arguing with him. I was sitting on the bathroom floor holding my nephew in tears. I looked at this sweet, innocent baby wondering how I could have put him in this situation. I told the operator I couldn't let my mom or the baby get hurt because of me. The operator told me the police were on the scene, but I was to remain in the bathroom. My mom called me letting me know the police were there and I could come out. I made it out of the bathroom to the doorway of the bedroom and could hear him cussing at the police. I started to walk down the hall, but the officer told me to wait until they had him secured in the car. My mom told me to put my nephew in his crib and then come talk to the police. The police asked me who he was, how did I know him, and if he was always like this. I answered every question truthfully. I could see him kicking the windows in the back of the police car. The officers kept yelling at him to stop, but he kept doing it. After everyone left I went to check on my nephew and then went back to the bathroom floor to cry. A few hours later, he used his one phone call to call me. Of course, he was threatening me and I just hung up. One of the police officers came back to check on us. I told the officer that he had used his one call to cal me. The officer told us the car was stolen and that he ended up kicking the glass out of the police car.

Memory Lane has much more turns, curves, potholes, speed bumps, stop signs and dead ends. However, the maintenance to repair and replace the broken areas has already begun. Sometimes the repairs don't feel so good to my flesh, but my spirit rejoices. As I exit Memory Lane, I'm learning to enjoy the journey to Happy Highway Hopeful Blvd, straight into the Holy of Holiest.

Memory 8-

This man had my mind so lost and twisted I routinely cleaned his nose out. He would lay on my lap and tell me to clean out his nose. I did exactly what I was told to do. Due to his cocaine addiction, he always had sores in his nose. One time, in particular, he woke me up in the middle of the night because his nose was bleeding so bad and he couldn't stop the bleeding. He started out with toilet paper, but the blood overflowed it. He tried a towel with no success. Finally, he grabbed a bed sheet. We had to get up and go to the emergency room. I remember as the doctor examined his nose he asked him if he did drugs. Of course, he said, "No," but I spoke up and said, "Yes." Maybe it was the fact that I was still half asleep that prevented me from noticing his anger. When the doctor stepped out of the room he said, "Bitch, what's wrong with you?" I was sitting in a chair in the corner with my head lying back against the wall. I jumped when I felt him kick my legs. I didn't want him to smash my head against the wall.

Memory 9-

At one time, we were in his mom's room watching TV and he fell asleep. The phone rang and I answered it only to hear a female ask to speak to him. I said, "He's asleep. Who is this?" I then said, "This is his girlfriend." She said, "His girlfriend? He told me you stayed with them because you had nowhere to go, but that you were not his girlfriend." I replied, "Okay," because honestly, it was not like I was losing something. I told her to hang on and told him to get up so he could take the call. He asked who it was and I told him. He grabbed the phone and argued with her about calling the house. I continued to watch TV since it didn't involve me. I could tell he was mad by the way he hung up the phone, but I figured if anybody should be mad it should be me. He got out of bed, stood in front of me and began punching me. He ended up knocking me down between the bed and wall. While I was down he stomped me saying, "Bitch, don't ever disrespect me like that." Mental abuse at its finest. I laid there until he pulled me up by my hair. He drug me across the bed standing me up while yelling in my face. At this point, he was face to face with me screaming, "Bitch if you ever do that again I will kill you. Why did your stupid ass do that?" I replied, "She called here, asked for you, so I woke you up." He immediately punched me saying, "And you're stupid enough to give me the phone?" He asked what we talked about and I told him. He punched me again because he felt like I was weak for not arguing with the girl. He knocked me sideways causing me to hit the floor. He stomped me on the side saying, "Bitch, this is what you get for being weak. Are you going to be weak again? Are you going to be funny and hand me the phone again?" In the midst of my tears, I got up so I wouldn't get hit again for crying. Once I was up he told me to go wash my face and make some lunch. I did exactly what I was told to do. I never got a chance to heal. Mental abuse is when you think you have escaped him by going to a relative's house and he shows up. I just so happened to be down the sidewalk at someone else's house when I got the phone call he was up there. They kept calling for me to come back because he was holding them at gunpoint. I knew he wouldn't shoot this particular cousin since he was how we met. Needless to say, I stayed at the neighbor's house all night until the guys from the neighborhood came back and showed their presence.

Memory 10-

Another time he showed up my other cousin and I was in the apartment when I heard a knock on the door. I opened the door without asking who it was only to see two 9mm's pointed in my face. He said, "Yeah bitch, it's me." I died on the inside. He started taking steps toward me telling me to back up. I saw his brother behind him. His brother quickly said, "I didn't come over here for all of this, I'll be in the car." As his brother walked off, he shut and locked the door. He asked me who was in the apartment.

I told him who was there and he instructed me to go get her. I went to the back bedroom, told her what was going on and that she needed to come into the living room. Of course, she didn't believe me. When we walked back in the living room he was still pointing both guns at us. He said, "Ya'll sit down and don't move." We sat on one couch and he sat on the other one across from us. My cousin kept saying, "Why the fuck are you doing this?" I had a picture of my son on the table and my cousin said to him, "How can you do this with your son's picture on the table?" He just looked at me because only he and I knew it wasn't really his son. In the beginning, when he was playing the role of my protector we decided it was better to say he was the daddy instead of admitting I had been raped. We sat there for what seemed like forever. My cousin kept calling him a punk and a coward. I told her to please be quiet, but she just kept on. She said if he was going to do anything he would have done it already. When she stood up, he cocked the gun and pointed it towards me. He told her if she moved he would shoot me. She looked back at me and sat down. He cocked the gun he had pointed at her and told me if I got up he'd shoot her. At this point, I just wanted to die. I didn't want to be responsible for her getting hurt. He just let us sit there. Every few minutes he would do say random things like, see what you make me do, I do this because of you, or you didn't think I would find you. I think my cousin lost some respect for me in the moment she turned to look for a response from me. I sat there still and quiet. My cousin said, "This is not her fault, it is your fault." He moved the guns closer to us on the table. We then heard someone turning the knob on the door. Over and over they kept trying to get in. The normal visitors knew during the day that the door was always unlocked. We both looked at him. I was nervous because I didn't want to be responsible for someone else getting hurt. When the person said, "What are ya'll doing? Open the door." Once I heard the voice I felt a little better. I had been out with the guy a couple of times and he held a high status. My cousin let the guy in, but I stayed still. He sat down in the chair beside me. He motioned for me to come sit in his lap. I directed my eyes to my ex who I noticed had put the guns under his shirt. He motioned me again. Once again I looked at my ex. Then the guy reached for my hand and guided me to his lap. I was terrified. I noticed my ex didn't do or say anything. My cousin said, "Shit, we have been sitting here all this time for nothing. I knew you were a coward." Once I saw that I leaned back on the guys chest and began talking to him. It was such a relief until someone else came in and told the guy he was needed outside. As soon as he went outside my ex said, "Bitch, I'm going to get you. I'm going to catch you when you come outside and push you down in the mud." He said this because it was raining and I had on all white. I said, "I'm not even going outside, plus the guy is right outside." My ex finally left. A few minutes later the guy came back in walking quickly. He asked me who that was that just left. I said it was my ex. My cousin yelled from the other room, "That's her baby daddy." The guy said, "If you want your baby to have a daddy then tell him he can't come over here anymore." I asked him what happened, but he just kept saying, "It's not a big deal, just call him and tell him what I said." We didn't have a phone so I walked down the hill to the pay phone. I knew my ex couldn't be home that quick and while I was standing by the pay phone my pager went off. I called the number back and it was my ex. He was at a store down the street from the apartment complex. I told him what I was in-structed to tell him and asked him what he did as he was leaving. He said, "Nothing, just raised my shirt up to let them know I was strapped." I could barely talk. He kept asking if I was with him and why I didn't want to be with him. I realized he wasn't acting in his normal tough way. I told him we were going out. He continued to ask why I didn't want to be with him. I said it was because of all the stuff he did to me and other people. I said, "I don't want to be around you, you're dangerous." He kept trying to tell me this new guy was worse than him, that he had heard stories about him. I told him he was wrong because this guy had been totally sweet to me and seeing a little fear in him about this new guy really made me like him that much more. I just gave my ex the message I was instructed to, hung up while he was trying to convince me this guy was worse than him. I walked back up the hill and we all went out later on that night. I eventually had to go back to my ex's family's house, but he didn't bother me at all. As a matter of fact, the new guy would drop me off and pick me up from there. One day my ex, his family and I were sitting in the living room. He was talking about me as bad as he could. I wasn't saying anything in response and then my pager went off. It was the new guy and I became very excited. I quickly called him back. He told me he was on his way to get me so I'd be ready. I jumped up excited. My ex was still sitting right there talking about me like I was worthless. His family asked me where I was going and who had called me. I told her, but she didn't believe me. She kept saying , "You're lying. Girl, how did you get him?" I said, "He approached me." My ex said, "She's not lying, and she doesn't want to be with me, but he's worse than I am." His family members said, "Oh, so you know about them being to-gether?" He hesitated to say yes but found a way to get it out. I heard the new guy pull up, so I told them bye and walked out the door. They were still in disbelief and came to the door to see if I was lying. When they realized I was telling the truth they laughed at my ex. They asked him what he was going to do now. I didn't wait around to see.

Things went back to the old way when I ended things with the new guy. I never saw any of the bad things my ex claimed the new guy did. I just realized it wasn't going anywhere and I couldn't keep using him as protection from my ex. As much as I tried to move around to prevent him from finding me, people I thought were on my side were telling him where I was. I don't know if it was for their protection or what, but at the time I couldn't understand it. One day, I was standing outside talking on the phone about being on the run from him. When I hung up I went to talk with some new friends relaxing on the steps. I felt relaxed because I thought he didn't know where I was and I knew these people didn't know either of us so they couldn't tell him. I went inside to use the bathroom, but when I came out I noticed the music was not playing anymore. As I reached the bottom step I saw a set of legs on the ground. I walked closer to get a better look and saw my ex standing in the middle of everybody holding a chrome and a black 9mm. I asked him what he was doing. He said, "I told you I would find you." He said he pulled up and asked them where I was at and which building I went in. He got angry because they said they didn't know. I tried to explain to him they weren't lying. He was so mad he pulled both guns on them and made them all get on the ground. He told me I had five minutes to get my stuff so we could go. He instructed one of the guys to get up and help me get my stuff telling him if it took to long he would start shooting people. As always I tried to apologize for my ex's actions. He was understandably upset and told me I seemed like a nice girl, but I could not be over there with this kind of problems. I agreed because I didn't want to be the cause of anyone getting hurt. When we walked out the door, I told him thank you and to stop talking to me for his own protection as we got closer. I got in the car, my ex walked backward and got in while pointing the guns at the others. When we left my ex laughed at how weak the people were for getting on the ground. I didn't think it was funny at all. He kept taunting me saying, "Ask me how I knew where you were at?" I just looked at him. At this point, I didn't care. It was clear I would never be able to escape him and the mental abuse. He grabbed my arm and demanded I ask him who told him where I was. Hearing the answer made me regret having to ask him. He laughed while I sat there puzzled. Confused as to how this could be happening; I am talked about for being with him, but when I leave people tell him where I am or he threatens to hurt someone close to me. The mental abuse had me trapped. I was damned if I did and damned if I didn't. I couldn't believe I had gotten into something this crazy.

Beat Down to Build Up

I remember the day my boss walked in the break room to hang the paper up. I saw it in his hand and the purple broken heart caught my attention. I went in there to read it and to my surprise, it was a flyer for a domestic violence class. I read it and laughed. A few days later while working, the Holy Spirit put that flyer before me again; however, this time, it wasn't funny at all. All I knew was that my past had caught up with my present, but I refused to let it meet my future. I knew it was time for me to deal with this and this was the group for me. I must be honest, it was easy to confess that until I thought about what I would have to face to deal with it. So many questions: Was I that unworthy of love, is that all I deserved, how could a person have that much anger and hate in the? Just the thought of dealing with this terrified me. I was scared of bringing everything back up. I actually found an excuse why I couldn't go to work on the issue. I put off going to the group the first week, yet I knew I was truly ready to be free and not just survive.

July 21, 2011, was a Thursday and I knew I was going to the group, but just the thought of having to possibly discuss what happened to me scared me so very bad. I remember being at work that day physically, but not mentally. My mind was in another place and the little stuff my staff had going on was nothing compared to the giant I challenged. As much as it scared me, it had been weighing me down and holding me back in life even more. Well, I got off work and decided to go straight to the group to be sure I found it; which was excuse #101. I found myself continuing to drive there while my mind was saying, "Girl, what are you doing? Go home!" As I reached the area I couldn't help but see it due to the huge sign. Big as day "Metropolitan Police Department Domestic Violence." I was like, "Are you serious?" It didn't stop there; the parking was facing a major street and interstate exit. "Exit," How great is that? I sat in the parking lot because I was an hour early. My boyfriend, at the time, called to be supportive; however, he was not actually doing that. Then I remembered a friend I could call. My friend got tired of me making excuses to leave and said, "Sheryl, please leave then, because you know you're going to." However, I knew myself and knew if I ever wanted to truly be free, I had to stay. I had a vision of me and my life staying the same if I chose to walk away and leave. As starting grew closer, my fear grew also. I nervously looked around at the few women who were there, thinking, "Do they really or did they really experience domestic violence?" All of the sudden I saw myself getting out of the car to go into the building which buzzed you in. I signed in and said, "I'm so nervous; it's my first time," but the lady was so nice I calmed down. The group leader thought she knew me, but I didn't recognize her. That totally embarrassed me. It turned out to be a small group which made me happy. The first time, the first day, the first exercise was called "House of Abuse" or as the group leader called it "House of Pain." It was a picture of a house divided up into squares. She told us to name each square with a type of abuse. I was ready to go at that point. To me, it felt like I would have to relive those moments to identify each type of abuse and the little exercise wasn't worth the hurt I was going to feel. I sat there stuck, wondering if others saw me and were wondering why I wasn't writing. I wrote physical at that moment because I wanted to get it over with. I was thinking to myself, "I hate this class and this isn't for me." Yet I stayed. When the group leader went to the board she asked us to name a type of abuse. Why did she call my name first? I only had one thing on my paper. As I answered, I wrote "yelling," because it was my warning of what he was about to do. What a warning sign! After that, I didn't talk until after class. I already felt a celebration within for just having made it to class. Look at me facing my giant.

The next day at work I found myself back in a place of fear.

There was a man who came there about a job, but he was acting very strange and aggressive. I handled the situation because my job title required this of me; however I was scared as ever. I ended up in a room, sitting in a chair with my back against the wall, so I could see everything coming my way. The lady in there with me asked me what was wrong. I tried to explain to her where my fear came from, but she wasn't understanding it. I summed it up by saying, "Girl, if my ex was right here and told me to smack you, I would slap slob out of your mouth." All she could say was, "Really?" Without hesitation, I told her I would apologize before I did it, but if I didn't do it, it would be worse on me.

I missed the next domestic violence group meeting because I didn't have any gas or gas money. I was hurt and upset because I so needed and wanted to be free. I knew this was only a trick of the devil to try and make me give up on freedom, but I'm still pushing forward. It's funny that I'm fighting to be free from this, but I know there is greatness tied to freedom.

Rage

When the rage is so raw, it makes you wonder, where did all this anger come from? What could I ever do to cause you to release that beast upon me? Could you imagine each blow brought another level of rage? What do you do when your body asks your heart, "Has he reached his limit?" How many levels of this could it possibly be?

My soul speaks up to comfort a bruised body and a broken heart, "Stay strong, keep standing. Heart, I know you are broken, but we can pick up the pieces." My body screams, "I CAN'T TAKE NO MO!" How can I stand up when his goal is to knock me down? (Yet the penalty for falling is getting stomped and pulled up by my hair.) If I stay down I'm sure to die. Damn, why did I get back up?

 When my heart finally decides to speak, it whispers, "Why can't I stop beating so he will stop beating me?" As strong as my soul tried to be, it secretly wondered how someone could hold so much hate. How could he beat the one who hugs him, kisses him, and without a doubt loves him? You see, it snuck in disguised as something beautiful, a protector, even love; however the ugliness of this rage could not be hidden for long. Only I was still strolling in the park of love and roses.

Imagine how I felt when he didn't recognize he was beating a bruised, already broken heart and body. Somewhere in the midst of an unpredictable guaranteed beating my soul cried out, "I don't know if there is a God, but if there is, please get him away from me."

Now I stand before you with Resurrection Life living on the inside of me, the brokenness of my heart made Whole, and a soul unashamed or fearful to Praise the One who responded to a question asked in secret. Maybe the day will come when rage sits in his cage and his soul secretly cries out.

Domestic Violence

Who gave it such a beautiful name?

Was it the person giving or receiving?

Better yet, could it have been someone on the outside looking in?

"Domestic Violence," Again I ask, "Who gave it such a beautiful name?

What part is beautiful?

Is it the hitting, punching, kicking, choking?

Maybe it's the side looks from spectators who'd rather stay out of it

Is it the looks on the faces of the children who want to protect me, but can't?

Somebody, please tell me who gave it such a beautiful name?

Maybe it was those officers who refused to take me serious because they couldn't see the bruises.

Tell me, was it the people who blamed me or called me stupid for staying, not realizing I'm already blaming myself and I'm staying to protect the people he said he'd kill if I left?

Somebody, please tell me who gave it such a beautiful name?

I know it didn't come from the person in the mirror, feeling, and looking ugly.

It didn't come from the one giving love only to get back hate.

Did anyone ever ask the person going through it to name it?

No, because then it wouldn't have been given such a beautiful name!

Fuss and Cuss

You fuss, you cuss,

You scream, you holla.

Every word comes harder and harder.

As bricks knocking against my soul,

I want to be whole.

Please don't throw another.

I'm trying to block them,

But my shield is just as hard as the bricks.

I need you to love me, hold me, encourage .me, cover me.

Not fuss, cuss, scream and holla at me.

Will I listen more, the louder you get?

Will I hide more, the harder it gets?

You couldn't hear my screams under yours.

Somebody help me! What did I get myself into?

Betrayal, a love affair that's killing my soul.

All I want to do is be whole.

Chapter 2

Pieces of Me

Given Too Soon

They don't even know I met you while I was broken in pieces; yet
you loved me!

I was lost and you came to find me.

From the first time you hugged me, I knew I was safe.

Broken and lost you held me together

You made sure I was seen as a queen!

They wonder why I love you so, but they don't know about the
night you held me close,

Sleeping on top of you was the only way that worked.

From the nights you woke up to find me in the bathroom,

To the nights you slept on the bathroom floor with me

You understood it all.

You kept me close as if we were one and we almost were.

You were my Big Daddy and I was your Fats.

A refreshing love, given too soon!

My wounds were too fresh to move,

But you carried me.

Though my layers of brokenness destroyed us, our nights in the bathroom kept us close.

No, they don't know but

But, I will always know how you loved my soul.

From the Chevy to the Van we were whole

You had my front and I had your back.

I was already drowning when you came out of nowhere to save me.

I was blind to see that you made me a better person.

My Lover-My Friend-given too soon!

I'm missing being by your side,

But we both know the lover never died!!!

Insight

"Given Too Soon" is about making a dangerous decision to move to the next step without first completing the previous step. This is even more necessary if there was any type of damage done in the previous situation. Sometimes I think emotional, mental, and spiritual healing is harder than physical healing. Not to mention, you can cover the physical hurt up, but no matter how much you try, the emotional, mental, and spiritual hurt have a way of coming out. Most of the time it comes out when you least expect it. It tends to come out on a person who has nothing to do with the cause of it. That's where I found myself at. A part of me knew I was too damaged from the emotional, mental, verbal, and physical abuse to be able to receive and reciprocate love. This new man in my life was totally different from what I was used to. No, he wasn't perfect or without fault, but he cared about me and loved me in a positive way. He was the first person I shared all my pain with, but he was also the one I released that pain on. I went from being abused to being the abuser. He never hit me back; he always walked away. I didn't understand the type of love he was giving me, so I took it as a sign of weakness. We endured a lot together, but my pain was deeper than he could reach. It took years for me to learn he was not created to carry the weight of my pain. It was not all bad between us, but I placed hurtful words and actions on him he didn't deserve.

Looking back on things, I realize I put him in a place that only God should have been in; however, in those days, I still wasn't sure if God really existed or would want to hear from me. Why would God want to hear from a girl who is only good enough to be abused? That's how deep satan had deceived my mind. I knew nothing about healing in that stage of life. At that time, I was just happy someone saw something attractive about me. I wish I could tell you, after years of this I learned to make better choices, but I didn't. I took the damage I already had, plus this new hurt and moved on. Just to be clear, I accepted full responsibility for my actions with this individual. This was growth in me and growth is a powerful thing.

Love

I have always heard people say things such as you've never been in love unless you've been hurt, love is pain, etc.... For the most part I believed this because it matched the events in my life until my sister introduced me to Christ. The Lord used the hardest, most painful thing in my life to minister to me. The first time I heard the Lord speak to me is when He said, "Ask Me to open your heart. You have purposely closed your heart." I was in a very broken place and had lost everything I thought I had, but God spoke to me. In the midst of my tears, laying in my nephew's bed, I cried out to the Lord and asked Him to please open my heart and He did just that! The Holy Spirit told me to turn to 1 John 4:8

"He who does not love does not know God. For God is love."

1 John 4:8

First, I didn't understand why God would want to use a sensitive subject with me. Then He showed me in the scripture that He is Love. He said, "Now read 1 John 4: 17-18

"Love has been perfected among us in this: that we may have boldness in the day of judgment; because as He is, so are we in this world.

1 John 4:17

"There is no fear in love; but perfect love cast out fear because fear involves torment. But, he who fears has not been made perfect in love."
1 John 4:18

In such a soft, sweet, and gentle manner the Holy Spirit said, "Hello, My Name is Love!" I cried even more because this was the total opposite of what I was told about or shown. Then He took it further and said, "Now, turn to 1 Corinthians 13:1-13." I couldn't understand why God would want me to read these typical "wedding scriptures." The Lord replied, "This is My character. Love is who I Am and this the character of Love."

1 Though I speak with the tongues of men and of angels, and have not charity, I am become as sounding brass or a tinkling cymbal.

2 And though I have the gift of prophecy, and understand all mysteries, and all knowledge; and though I have all faith, so that I could remove mountains, and have not charity, I am nothing.

3 And though I bestow all my goods to feed the poor, and though I give my body to be burned, and have not charity, it profiteth me nothing.

4 Charity suffereth long, and is kind; charity envieth not; charity vaunteth not itself, is not puffed up,

5 Doth not behave itself unseemly, seeketh not her own, is not easily provoked, thinketh no evil;

6 Rejoiceth not in iniquity, but rejoiceth in the truth;

7 Beareth all things, believeth all things, hopeth all things, endureth all things.

8 Charity never faileth: but whether there be prophecies, they shall fail; whether there be tongues, they shall cease; whether there be knowledge, it shall vanish away.

9 For we know in part, and we prophesy in part.

10 But when that which is perfect is come, then that which is in part shall be done away.

11 When I was a child, I spake as a child, I understood as a child, I thought as a child: but when I became a man, I put away childish things.

12 For now we see through a glass, darkly; but then face to face: now I know in part; but then shall I know even as also I am known.

13 And now abideth faith, hope, charity, these three; but the greatest of these is charity.

1 Corinthians 13:1-13

I was amazed to learn the true identity of Love. I would have to say, I like this a whole lot better. Now the question is, how do I apply this to my life? I had to read it daily, sometimes multiple times a day. I had to make the choice to block out what people kept trying to tell me about love and stand on what God told me. No, it wasn't easy, because people really try to force things or their own way on you. I experienced the results of people's love, so what did I have to lose by trying God's love? As childish as it may seem, I would get in front of the mirror and confess, "Yes, Jesus Love Me and I receive that love; it is okay to love and be loved." Many times that brought me to tears, but what hurt the most was the fact that I really didn't believe it. It took a while before I actually started believing it, but I never stopped confessing it. As time progressed and I grew closer to Christ, I learned that perfect means complete and mature. I knew in my spirit this Love was real and so much better! Don't continue to be deceived by the enemy.....Love is Truly Beautiful!

"There is something to be

Thankful for in every situation!

You just have to choose

To see it!"

The Ultimate Yes Girl

Yes, you can get these goods!

Yes, you can run in and out of my house and my life, whenever it's convenient for you!

Yes, I will cook, clean, and dance for you!

Yes, I will take your verbal abuse!

Yes, I will shine on point for you!

Yes, I will hold that pistol and pack for you!

Yes, I will let you disrespect me and not expect better!

Yes, I will have your back while you let me hit the ground!

Yes, I will work and pay bills so you don't have to be responsible!

Yes, I will say no to me, my family, my future, my hopes, and dreams, so I can be your Ultimate Yes Girl!

Yes, I will cry silently when you break my heart!

Yes, I will call others when I need encouragement because all you do is discourage me!

Yes, I will defile the temple of God just to put a smile on your face!

Yes, I will lower my expectations so I won't be as hurt when you let me down!

Yes, I will be a less than underachiever so I can be your Ultimate Yes Girl!

Yes, I will love you more than I love myself!

Yes, I will put myself in a place of bondage to help you get free!

Insight

"The Ultimate Yes Girl" was written June 23, 2012, at 1:39 A.M. This was a season in my life when I wasn't very happy with myself. I thought I had made such big changes in my life which would prevent me from making the same decisions when choosing a mate. I thought, this time, would be different, but I found myself in another mess. It wasn't an abusive relationship, but it definitely wasn't headed in a positive direction. The inner battle for me was trying to figure out how I got here. I couldn't figure out how someone working, spending time with family and friends, and active in church could go back down the same road. I thought because I was active in church, reading scripture faithfully, confessing the Word of God over my life, and didn't' drink or go to clubs that there was no way I could make the same mistake. I allowed myself to be put in situations that could have changed my life drastically. I had gotten so deep into this relationship, I began turning against family and friends who had something negative to say about it. There would be times I would walk away from the relationship saying, "I can't live like this, I gave up this fast lifestyle a long time ago." The pain of being separated from him was sometimes too much, so I would go back. I eventually learned that temporary pain is easier to deal with than long term pain.

On June 23, 2012, at 7:51 P.M. the Holy Spirit responded to The Ultimate Yes Girl. The Holy Spirit said, "For everything you say no to, I say yes to you. There is power in your words; including "No." You have believed and accepted deception, which caused you to say "Yes" to the things of the world and "No" to things of the Word.

Locked Up!

You did the crime, but I'm doing the time! Though you put your-self there, I'm the one carrying the load. Everyone has been the blame; from the white man to the P.O...... Keep money on the phone, on your books, send packages, come to visit, write you, send some stamps, send some pictures. Why do you sound like that? Really? Do you have to ask? I forgot that in spite of all I'm doing, you consider it nothing because you're the one doing the time. Your actions put you behind bars, but your words and ac-tions put me behind them. Grateful for nothing; asking for every-thing, yet you refuse to accept that no one owes you anything. This is your payment and reward for your actions and mine for choos-ing you. How can I be wrong because I break bad to live my life? You choose not to acknowledge that life, excitement, family, etc...., do not exist in your world. I wouldn't understand because I'm a free world person, but truth is, I just released myself from the sen-tence my choice gave me.

You, locked up by choice, didn't have to do what you did and I don't have to stay. However, I'm the one that is looked down on because I choose not to suffer your consequences with you. The sentence came in, nothing made sense. I no longer matter, it's all about you. Killing myself, depressed, and fed up trying to make it happen for you. All you do is complain it's not happening fast enough or happening how you want it to. Yeah, you're locked up, but I'm doing the time.

You, hard and maintaining with your boys, but whining with me. You think living a double life is hard? What about this double sentence I received? I forgot you're the one locked up, so I don't matter. Doesn't matter what I have to do, just answer the phone when you call. I'm tired of hearing her tell me my account is low and add money if I want to continue to get these calls. You question me about money but are fine with what I spend on you. Save money, put some up, but first, make sure you put some money on the phone, put some money on my books, send me a package, come to visit, write me, send me some stamps, and some pictures.

Well, I'm taking a stand! I'm breaking bad because of me....Not Jody!

The truth is you're locked up because of your choices, so don't pass your sentence to me. Jumping out of the car doesn't make me real, but leaving me here to handle everything on these streets makes you, what?

Yeah, you did the crime, but I did the time!

Holding It Down

Yeah, if I do say so myself, I was holding it down better than most.

Taking chances for the sake of shining.

Making it happen, that's all that matters.

The silent partner to the side just happens to be the CEO

Taking losses we couldn't afford, but we always bounced back.

Borrowed a few times and made it back to the top, Mad at some of the choices, so I made a Boss Lady move

In spite of what I you thought, it turned out to be the right choice.

We were holding it down so good, we forgot to hold each other; you good at what you do, but I make you better.

They scream your name for what they think you have, but I scream your name for you; for what I know you're made of.

For the hugs, that refreshed us when you came through the door

For the kiss that we hoped never ended at 2:45

All that holding down and the most valuable thing slid through both our hands!

Beautiful

How does something so Beautiful turn into something so ugly?

From making a jukebox on the phone to doing a hundred on the highway.

Being from two different parts of the world, we came together and just fit....

From the first kiss to the last diss, my mind is full of you!

From prepaid calls to green dot, we were all in.

Man, how did something so Beautiful turn into something so ugly?

From loving me to loving you; yet we lay with others.

From max visit to the Big V. G., but somehow back behind the glass we made it work

From breaking bad to holding it down, we were solid

Then please tell me, how did something so Beautiful turn into something so ugly?

From the Don on the block to the King of the streets and your kingdom didn't include me

So was it real? It was in that moment. A four and a half year moment, but......

From the tatt on my back to the tatt on your chest

Forever you'll be in my heart.

Lady of Elegance

As a Lady of Elegance, I walk in the royalty given to me by The King of Kings. I boldly walk in that authority as a Lady of Elegance. I am a Lady of Elegance in how I talk. I speak words of Life and Edification. I am a Lady of Elegance in my behavior. I walk in a place of high calling, my good will never be spoken evil of. I am a Lady of Elegance in my appearance. I represent The King of Kings, therefore I will always show His Excellence. I am a Lady of Elegance in how I serve. I will not wait on God by doing nothing, but I will wait on Him as a waiter, by serving. I will put my hands to the plow and be God's hands extended. I am a Lady of Elegance in my love walk. I know that love is beautiful and it is more than okay for me to love and be loved. Love is an action word and I will see the fruit in it. I am a Lady of Elegance because I am complete in Christ.

Insight

The Holy Spirit gave me *"Lady of Elegance"* at a time in my life when I felt the total opposite. A few months previously I wrote *"The Ultimate Yes Girl"* and it was an eye opener to my actions when it came to men. I was shocked, ashamed, and confused. I definitely couldn't understand how I could be like this and the Lord still call me a Lady of Elegance. I've been told by people what a lady does and how she acts, but I've never been told what being a lady really means. As if that wasn't enough, you add "elegance" to it! I truly didn't know what it meant to be elegant. I decided not to let the fear of the unknown stop me or keep me stuck in something I wasn't created to be in. When the One who created you is telling you your true identity, then you clear your ears, heart, and spirit and listen up. No, it wasn't and still isn't easy, but I know Jesus loves me. I know Jesus only wants His best for me. If He brought this to my attention then He brought the answer with it. I'm doing this! Well, I thought I was. I can honestly admit I messed up as soon as I started, but I kept moving forward. Does this mean I am completely there? I answer you in the faith of Christ with a joyful, "Yes!" In order for things to manifest, you must first believe, then begin to walk in it, as if it is already so.

Part of being a Lady of Elegance my attire speaks volumes. What I choose to wear voices both who I am and what I am clothed with within. Learning to adjust my attire based on the standard of who I am in Christ and not the standard of the culture was a battle. Was I prepared to be looked at funny, talked about or just simply be an outcast? I didn't want to experience or be any of that; until I realized that looking like everyone only gave me the reward of being like everyone else. It didn't add up because I knew I was created to be different, to stand out, to be unique. Now, I get dressed for me. I enjoy letting my outside attire tell you how loved, glorious and blessed I am within.

Why was I shocked to find out a Lady of Elegance doesn't talk the way I do? Lord, what are you doing to me? No, what did I pray about? I already changed my attire, now I'm about to change the way I talk. How will people handle this? Here we go again! Will they look at me funny, talk about me, or just simply make me an outcast? Either way, I'm moving forward. I enjoyed the rewards of the last process, so let's do it! For me, the funniest part was catching myself in mid-conversation talking the old way. Sometimes I would giggle to myself, sometimes I would get frustrated, let it slide, or deal with the issue once I was calm. I can honestly say, just letting it slide did not bring me joy. I went from cursing every time I opened my mouth to being quiet. I would get mad a lot of times when I didn't say anything but felt like cussing someone out for justification. I often heard myself asking, "If you said that, would it honor God?" The times I talked in my old ways got me nowhere. The Holy Spirit would correct me, remind me of what I was doing, and why. If I did offend someone, after repenting to God, I would go back to that person and apologize. A simple "I'm sorry" was not my new standard. I examined myself, identified where I was wrong, and let them know the steps made or was making to correct it.

My goodness, now my attitude! Sheryl, what have you prayed for girl? I have known for years my attitude is based on the things that have happened to me. My attitude came from a place of defense. I was tired of being hurt so I determined it wasn't going to keep happening. The sad thing is trying to control everything just made me angrier. The fact it wasn't working didn't matter because I kept trying it. All it did was produce more anger. Other people thought I was mad at them, but I was honestly mad at myself. It's horrible how we treat ourselves while claiming to love others. I refuse to stay the same! I went from being this "in your face, I'm not taking this," type of girl to speechless. This level was another battle for me. I felt like I was letting people walk all over me. I hadn't learned how a Lady of Elegance responds to such things. I had to cry out to the Lord so much, just to stand when I wanted to fall. People thought I was losing it or having a meltdown, but I knew it was the total opposite. I call it my growing pain season. Now I look back on it and realize it was all for the benefit of the greater purpose of God.

The Broken Fighter

What happens when the fighter doesn't have another fight in them? Yet they are scheduled for much more and the ones that seem to be taking him out are the unexpected battles.

No time to recover and training doesn't exist.
Would it be better to just stay in the ring; after all, you know as soon as you get out, it's time to get back in.

I can't tell if these are different battles or I'm taking one long beating. Somehow I keep getting up. I can't handle another fight.

However, the brokenness in me keeps trying to mend itself back together. In the midst of the blows, damage after damage, blow after blow. I'm a broken fighter looking for a refuge.

Blossoming Flower

My beautiful flower! So delicate, yet so strong. Beauty and strength covered by petals of confusion. What layer must I remove first? Shall it be the rape, of your soul and mind? Shall it be the lack of self-esteem, making you question why I created you? Shall it be the doubt, whether I will really heal the brokenness? Shall it be the confusion, driving you back to where I freed you from? Shall it be the lack of attention, making you feel invisible in a crowded room? Shall it be the desperation, making you settle for anything? Shall it be the feeling of lacking love, which is already there, but somehow seemed to make it the root of the problem? Love covered by all the dirt. Shall I pluck away the petals or remove the dirt? How about I rain down on you?

Love,

Jesus

Actions Versus Love?

If I constantly give myself away the moment I need me, does that mean I don't love you? The guilt of letting you down drives me to please you and seek your happiness. I can't let you down, even though the strain of this load is killing me. Which is worse; letting you down or being crushed by the weight of the load? Truthfully, I would rather the load take me out than the reaction of me letting you down.

In the beginning, I did everything out of love, but somehow it turned into fear and obligation. Even though I need a moment for me, I can't take it because it would mean I didn't love you. Suck it up is all I can say. If I love you more and harder will it one day cause you to give me that same measure of love? That's a strong, "No!"

Does anyone love like me? If it doesn't look like the love I give does that mean it's not love? How could we have twisted such a marvelous thing as love? Why do we make it so complicated? Nonetheless, will it change the fact I'm exhausted and depressed trying to love you? Is that really love?

I Miss You

I miss you! We used to hang out together, all the time. Never was one seen without the other. No one understood our relationship, but we knew we made each other stand out. The best friend I ever had; now I barely see you. The sad thing is, it took a while before I realized you were gone. Every time I thought you were back it turned out to be your cousin. Y'all resemble so but still y'all are not the same. No disrespect to Giggles, but I miss my best friend, Laughter. I blamed everybody and everything for you leaving until I realized I drowned you with my tears.

If I Knew Where

Sometimes I see you and you're bright, fire red and beating louder than an entire drum line. Sometimes I see you and you're like a five thousand piece puzzle and all the pieces are scattered throughout an ongoing maze; never knowing which time is when. I never take the first step to come and find you. If I ever decided to go get you, would I have the answers you were looking for? What if those answers were the secret code to get you back? Where did I lose you at? At what point did I give you away? Who has you? Will they give you back? How do they treat you? Did they love you or abuse you? Where can I find you at? Will you give me a clue? Who has you? Will they let you speak or do they have you in such a web of bondage that only they can maneuver through? Have you tried to find me and come back to me? Or must I find you? Why is it taking so long? Could it be that my fear of the first step is stronger than my yearn for you? Who has separated us? Did they know how fragile you are? Was I not protecting you good enough? I wonder if they acted like they cared, just long enough for me to drop my guard, so they could take you? Who knows? All I know is I miss you. Who knew life choices would be so hard without you. I thought a few people came to help me find you, but it didn't work out. Some were sent to push us further apart; others I think I pushed away out of fear of rejection. Would you want me after all this time? I couldn't handle the rejection. At times I feel like you're here and then with the next call, the next text, or the next action you're gone. I'm struggling because I don't want to lose you, but coming to get you cost a high price. I know you're worth it, but I have to believe it enough to do it. If I came to get you, which time would it be? The bright red or the maze? How do I tell my family, my friends, and God Almighty that I lost my heart? If I knew where my heart was at, would I go get it?

The Source

Where is the source of my ink? If I began sharing what's on my mind and heart I don't want to stop. My head is banging, my eyes are blurry, is it my blood pressure or my life? I want to scream, I want to cry, I want to run, I want to hide, I want to love, I want to be loved, I want a hug, I want to be hugged.

I want to...I want to...I want to stop being confused. It seems like every situation I get n turns into a place of bondage; a place I lose myself, lose my identity and take on the identity of others. Others are the same people who tell me to be myself.

Random thought.....

If my life stops hurting, will my heart stop hurting? Maybe then my head will stop hurting. Why in trying to live my life, am I worried about people? Everybody expects me to do the same thing. I found myself in a stable dying place with people who want to keep me there, yet screaming, "Get out, get up, Sheryl!"

I want to breathe! I want to live!

I have to keep pushing, but that's easier said than done. Considering I gave up my fight a very long time ago, all I have is my faith.

Not yours, hers, his, or anyone else's, but by

My faith in Christ!

Twisted

I'm all twisted up in this tornado of situations. I watched the news all night and no one alerted that it was coming. It's coming through reckoning havoc. Picking up my home and twisting it until everything is out of order. It threw my car into someone else's possession, as if it didn't matter; crushed my hopes and dreams. It blew through my mind as if my thoughts were vapors. Lost and lonely, who can find me in this tornado? I'm not where I used to be nor do I know where I will end up. When it's over, will you be able to identify me or will I be able to identify my belongings? Help me find something that will tell me who I am because I'm all twisted up in this tornado of situations.

"Even in the midst

Of a storm

God always sends

An umbrella!"

No Complaints

No complaints, no concerns. I'm just happy to be me!

To be able to laugh with my family is a gift from above.

Blessed beyond measure to hug my son, to go to work, and enjoy what I do; having the strength to go work this body out.

You see, though I have seen much, I still have neither complaints nor concerns.

I know my value.

I know the cost of a smile, a giggle, and yes, even the cost to stand.

Who am I to cheat Him, to rob Him of His creation, His Love, and His Joy?

For all that He has given me, I humbly return His Love, Joy, and Peace.

I'm just happy to be me!

Meant to Fly

This bird has always been meant to fly; soaring far above the distractions that try to keep her from her greater destination. Flowing in the gentle breeze of the wind to the next scene. Admiring the warmth of the Son that wakes her for the new journey ahead. Flying with purpose, to purpose, for a purpose; each time higher and further! Only resting on the Tree of Life.

This bird has always been meant to fly!

Being beautiful and unique makes distinct in all her ways. To take care of her, you must know the Word from the manual used to create her. She is delicate and sleek.

Her vision is one of limitless possibilities. She's rarely seen because the road she travels is narrow and few can find it. She rises early to prepare, so not only will her nest be extraordinary, but her reserve as well. She is flying beautifully and free that you may see; it was always meant to be!

Chapter 3

Spirit Fuel

A Father's Love

A Father's love is the foundation in which I stand on. The covering which protects me and the strength that pulls me through. It's the hug that makes everything okay. It's the phone call that brightens my day. It's the love that never goes away. A Father's love is what gives me the courage to face tomorrow. It teaches me change is possible. Though we make mistakes, embrace the opportunity to correct it.

Confuse Defeat

You thought you won and by the looks of things you did. Every time I got back up, you knocked me down. Who's winning, me or you? I'm confused because my heart says you, but my spirit says me. So I've decided to turn it around and confuse defeat. Situation says defeat; Holy Spirit says Victory. You say give up, but Victory says I'm just getting started. Another trial, another test...just give up, you've been defeated. Not so fast, I see it now, another ribbon, another medal and I just tied my shoes to endure this race. You won't win defeat because I am already in a place of Victory. Confuse me no more, to think of giving up. It's not an option. Victory is my name! I smile when I should cry. I stand up when I should hide. I run when you tell me to crawl. I build when you try to knock down. I am Victorious! I know you thought you won and by the looks of things, you did. Until...I confused defeat by standing stable in my Victory! I am Victorious!

415

I'm surrounded by 5 ways of escape.

The ability to run into grace and new opportunities await me.

The view is beautiful, but it hurts so bad. I see what could be, but what stands between us seems impossible to achieve.

It turns out what I thought I was locking out has caused me to be locked in.

Oh, to be surrounded by 5 ways of escape, but not know how to get out is unspeakable!

The 4 post that protects the creation of 1 is refreshing; as the covering of Grace, Goodness, and Favor hovers over.

My view is enlightened, I take the steps and realize the key was in the door the whole time!

His Polish

The more you polish me the cleaner I get. How do you know my ability to shine if you refuse to let me endure the process?

Dare to dip me in the solution so I may reach the resolution.

A brush here, a brush there, working out what doesn't belong. It's along the stones that seem to be so wrong.

Beautiful and ugly; puzzling to the eye.

Underneath you see so clear is the ability to shine brightly as the morning star.

Dare to dip me in the solution so I may reach the resolution.

Maybe the false concept that this is a competition is clouding your vision. Maybe the pride you hold is truly old or just maybe you know this shine I hold is bright and bold. Maybe it's not to be told.

How do you determine my ability to shine without even letting me endure the process? It didn't break through in your time frame, but shame on me because you changed the game. Below the ugliness and dirt, I'm screaming, "The shine is here. Don't give up!" Yet my ability to shine was never destroyed by what appeared to prevail.

You counted me out too soon. It was the Lord's will I be healed from each wound. Although you refused to let me endure the process, it didn't stop my shine. You just couldn't or better yet, wouldn't see it.

Now I know it wasn't the more you polish me, but the more He polishes me that I became clean, pure as snow, and made new! So I'm forever grateful for the obstacles you created that The Creator may show Himself Greater!

More Than A Title

Seems like it just hit me that being a Christian is more than a title; it's more than following the crowd. What happens when you wake up to realize that's exactly what you've been doing? The maze of trying to figure out how you got here has you spinning in circles. No, this isn't the voice that called me. How did I get the voice telling me to kill myself mixed up with the voice that tells me to live in Him? How? How? How did I end up spinning in circles? I followed what I thought was Him, until the one I followed led me to destruction. Now I'm wondering, how did I get the voice telling me to give my body away mixed up with the voice that says honor your body, for it is the temple of the Holy Ghost? I'm trapped, there's no way out. I heard that voice telling me to give up, but this time, I heard His voice loudly say, "I will never leave you nor forsake you." I giggle to myself, I didn't get them mixed up this time! His voice guided me out, gives me instructions on how to stay out, and now I have to walk it out, talk it out, and live it out, so I can give it out. This is not the end, but simply a pause, a rest, a refreshing! You see, being a Christian is more than a title, it's more than following a crowd, but is being an imitator of Christ; even in the smallest of areas. That one day, you may hear His voice say, "Well done, my good and faithful servant."

Natural and Spiritual Cleaning

"How natural cleaning lines up with spiritual cleaning"

Isaiah 38:1

1 Corinthians 14:33—

I need to get organized, not just naturally in my home, but in my spirit as well.

Matthew 18:18

If I allow my natural house to be unorganized and filthy, how much does that say about my spiritual house?

Just like you can spread germs naturally, you can spread unclean spirits. Smith Wigglesworth stated that the Holy Spirit comes when a person is cleansed.[1] There must be a purging of the old life.

> Purge— to remove impurities and other elements by or as if by cleaning. To rid of sin, guilt or defilement.

Malachi 3:3—

Allowing God to purge you puts you in a position of righteousness, then you can offer your life to God in righteousness, not just trying to give money.

When we have been cleansed and choose not to walk in *Joshua 1:8,* we fall into *Matthew 12:43-44.* Not only is it 7 times stronger to you, but whatever you're connected to as well.

[1] The Anointing by Smith Wigglesworth

*Matthew 10:1—*Just like you have the power to go out and buy chemicals to clean your house, you have been given Power over unclean spirits.

Certain chemicals are for certain areas; for instance, you wouldn't use toilet bowl cleaner in your kitchen. So if believing the Lord for healing, then you would need scriptures for healing.

All chemicals have a "kill time." It has to stay on the surface a certain amount of time to fulfill its purpose.

2 Peter 3:8—

Tells us we can't rush God because His timing is not ours.

Hebrews 4:12—

Tells us the Word reaches even the unclean.

All chemicals have instructions, but it's up to you to read and follow them as it instructs us in *Colossians 3:12-17*

While you are cleaning your natural house, allow God to clean your spiritual house.

Remember this is all "Because He first loved us." *1 John 4:19*

*This was my very first Bible study lesson I unexpectedly shared with the church congregation. Needless to say, everyone was shocked, but not as much as me. Even then I was very aware that due to the actions of my life people don't expect God to use me. It was amazing yielding to the Holy Spirit and just letting Him move. As I finished, I remember my sister standing up in the back right corner saying, "Y'all better listen to her! Y'all don't understand who that is coming through. I know where she has been, so I know what it took for her to get this and allow God to use her." That's my sister! Jesus, I felt so special! So, it was not a question that this would be in the book.

Confessions

Encourage Yourself

Many times we depend on other people to speak words that will strengthen and encourage us, however, you are the best person for that. Learning how to encourage yourself is one of the most powerful things you can learn and do. The moment no one is answering the phone or even willing to lift you up; this is the moment knowing how to speak over your life, your situation, and your body will manifest itself. It may be a problem of speaking the wrong thing over your life, your situation, your body, etc... Does what you say about you line up with what God says about you? Just in case you're not sure, I'm pleased to share some scriptures which have helped me and confessions the Holy Spirit has given me.

Forgiveness

Galatians 5:1 — "I will stand fast in the liberty wherewith Christ has mad me free and I will not be entangled again with the yoke of bondage."

Ephesians 4:32— "And be ye kind one to another, tenderhearted, forgiving one another, even as God in Christ forgave you."

Mark 11:25-26— "And when ye stand praying, forgive, if ye have ought against any; that your Father also, which is in Heaven may forgive you your trespasses. But, if ye do not forgive, neither will your Father which is in Heaven forgive you trespasses."

Acts 8:22— "Repent therefore of thy wickedness and pray God, if perhaps the thought of thine heart may be forgiven thee."

Isaiah 65:16— "That he who blesseth himself in the earth shall bless himself in the God of truth; and he that sweareth in the earth shall swear by the God of truth, because the former troubles are forgotten and because they are hid from mine eyes."

Confession

"Father God, I come humbly before You in the name of Your Son, Jesus Christ. Lord, I come repenting for the unforgiveness I have been holding onto concerning _____. I know Your Word says, if I can't forgive, then You can't forgive me and I don't want that to happen. I need the strength and help to forgive _____ and let it go. I plead the Blood of Christ over this unforgiveness towards _____ and thank You that I walk in forgiveness toward _____. Father, I ask that You touch _____'s heart that _____ might be able to forgive me as well. In Jesus' name, I pray. Amen. Amen means I agree, so be it.

Confession of Thanks

Praise you Christ, my Messiah! You woke me up this morning, in the right frame of mind, body functioning properly, in a bed, in a house with lights, water, and food and then blessed me to get in a car with gas to go to a job! Praise You, my Messiah! I am overflowing in blessings and life only because of and through You. Thank You, Jesus! Thank You for all You have done for me. Thank You for the Holy Spirit who continues to teach me, guide me, comfort me, hold me, and so much more. Thank You, Jesus! When I don't show thankfulness the Holy Spirit will quicken me to repent and remind me of my many blessings. Jesus, thank you for loving me and showing me how to love You!

God blessed me to see this day, so I choose to make it a great one! By the power of the Holy Spirit inside of me, I walk in love, grace, favor, mercy, and peace. The blood of Christ covers me and protects me from any hurt, harm, or danger physically as well as spiritually. The strong and mighty warring angels are encamped around my family keeping them safe from any hurt, harm, or danger physically, as well as spiritually. Now because of the Power and Authority was given to me by Jesus Christ, I face this day in liberty and victory. Satan is defeated and has no power in or over my life or my family's life. I stand because Jesus Christ is Lord of my life. In Jesus Name Amen!

Jesus Loves Me!

When Discomfort Becomes Comfortable

Matthew 8:34 & Galatians 4:9

As people, we can unexpectedly and unintentionally get comfortable in discomfort. Example: How we keep our home. We chose to tell our company, "Excuse the mess, etc..." We have become comfortable living in a mess instead of cleaning up behind ourselves. I'm sure once the house is nice and clean you enjoy it more and the atmosphere is calmer. Why not experience that all the time?

In Matthew 8:28-33 two demon-possessed men saw and recognized Jesus. As you continue to read, you learn there was a witness who ran to tell what happened. One would think the people would celebrate two demon-possessed men are now free, but in verse 34, the whole city begged Jesus to leave. Wow! The Truth and Liberty in your city, in your presence and you beg Him to leave. That's what we still see today. We all have loved ones we desire to be free, but we can't figure out why they would stay where they're at.

Truth is, some simply are comfortable there and don't want to come out, but rather Christ come in. As believers, we have to make the choice daily, hourly, minutes, or even seconds not to go back to what's familiar. Even though it didn't feel good we got used to the pain. Comfortable in an uncomfortable place!

Galatians 4:9— "But now after you have known God, or rather are known by God, how is it that you turn again to weak and beggarly elements, to which you desire again in bondage?"

You have been made free by Christ. What or who could be that good to make you want to go back?

I encourage you not to beg Jesus to go *(Matthew 8:34)*, but to get comfortable in freedom. Meditate and confess *Galatians 5:1* making it personal.

Galatians 5:1—"I will stand fast therefore in the liberty by which Christ has made me free and I will not be entangled again with the yoke of bondage."

Be Empowered to Prosper! Jesus Christ is Lord and His banner over you is Love!

Ezekiel 11:5— "And the Spirit of the Lord fell upon me and said upon me, '"Speak," thus saith the Lord; Thus have ye said, O house of Israel: for I know the things that come into your mind, every one of them."

Romans 12:2— "And be not conformed to this world: but be ye transformed by the renewing of your mind, that ye may prove what is that good, and acceptable, and perfect will of God."

Ephesians 4:23-24— "And be renewed in the spirit of your mind; and that ye put on the new man, which after God is created in righteousness and true holiness."

2 Timothy 1:7— "For God has not given us the spirit of fear; but of power, of love, and a sound mind."

Philippians 2:5—"Let this mind be in you, which was also in Christ Jesus."

Confession

Father God, I come to You in the name of Your Son Jesus Christ. Thanking You that I have a sound mind. I bind the spirit of double-mindedness and confusion. I plead the powerful Blood of Christ over my thoughts and mind. I thank You that I think on things that are true and of a good report. I thank You for peace in my mind. I thank You that I have the mind of Christ and I meditate on the Word of God, day and night. In Jesus Name, Amen and Amen mean I agree, so be it!

Exposing Deception

We have all experienced some form of rejection in our lives. However, the Truth of the matter is we were created by God and when we were separated from Him, He sent Jesus Christ to redeem us.

Reject/Rejection— means to throw back, to refuse, to disown.

Whether the rejection was from family, friends, or a job it hurts just the same. As a result of carrying rejection, we try to protect ourselves. Normally this causes us to isolate ourselves. However, we don't have to stay that way. The Word of God tells us Jesus Christ is our Redeemer. *(Titus 2:13-14)*

Redeem/Redeemer— means to repurchase, to win back, to free from what distresses or harms.

Jesus Christ is someone who redeems. He is also our example that we can be healed from the deception rejection brings. In *Isaiah 53:5* you will read how Jesus Himself experienced rejection. Yet He continued to fulfill the purpose for which He came.

Isaiah 53:5 tells us that by His stripes we were healed. That healing is not just physical, but any part of you that is broken *(Psalm 147:3)* Allow the Truth *(John 14:6)* to expose deception so you can walk in total freedom *(Galatians 5:1)*.

Has the rejection from others tainted your view of God desiring you? Are you willing to release deception and embrace The Truth? Well, today I challenge you to make the decision to walk in the freedom Christ has given you.

Note From the Author

Well, the secret is out, I like to write. To me writing is a form of escape and releasing. I have experienced many test and trials in my life. Yes, some may have knocked me down, but they didn't take me out. I'm not ashamed of the things I have been through, but I am grateful. I'm grateful I learned valuable lessons and was saved for such a higher purpose. I have shared moments of my life, but it still doesn't describe who I am. I could be described as:

The Molested Girl

The Rape Victim

The Adolescent Mother

The Abuse Victim

The Gangster's Girlfriend

There are a lot of choices to choose from. I made it through those situations and quite a few more. I've learned those situations do not determine who I am. It's what I went through, but it's not who I am. So I will describe myself from a place of Victory, a place of Freedom *(Galatians 5:1)*. I love the Lord Jesus Christ and I have an awesome relationship, with Him. Because of that relationship I am strong, I am a fighter! I love to encourage others! I love to laugh! I am a giver! I'm blessed to be a wife, mother, daughter, sister, aunt and a friend. Most of all, I am an Overcomer, I am Victorious!

About the Author

LaSheryl Frazier was born in Nashville, TN. She received her education in the public school system, only to drop out from a local High School. At the age of 28, she obtained her GED. After years of working in the restaurant industry LaSheryl began a successful journey in the healthcare field. She briefly had her own residential cleaning service. In the early 2000's, LaSheryl joined a local church that encouraged journaling, which awakened a hidden gift inside of her. The desire to write prevailed against the destruction of her past. Through the years LaSheryl not only began to write again but also save them and share them with others. Her local church home not only helped her write again but first and foremost taught her how to fight in the spirit. With this new way of living LaSheryl is able to speak into the lives of family members, friends, children, teenagers, young adults, co-workers and others as their paths cross. The life experiences that she overcame gives her the courage to help others out of it or prevent them from experiencing it. Although LaSheryl desires to travel she still resides in Nashville, TN.

To Contact LaSheryl for speaking engagements or to order more copies of her book email her at

lasheryl.d.35@gmail.com

www.ingramcontent.com/pod-product-compliance
Lightning Source LLC
Chambersburg PA
CBHW060129050426
42448CB00010B/2039